While every precaution has been taken in the preparation of this book, the author and publisher assumes no responsibility for errors or omissions, or for damages resulting from the use of the information contained herein. Some names and identifying details have been changed to protect the privacy of individuals.

SURVIVING TOXIC IN-LAWS: THE BIG BULLIES

First edition. May 1, 2018.

Copyright © 2018 Miriam Davids.

Written by Miriam Davids.

Dedicated to all individuals that had to survive and endure mistreatment during their marriage at the hand of their toxic In-laws and those still stuck in a pretty negative relationship with their in-laws. This guide helps to turn every bad and unbearable situation into a positive one.

~Table of Contents~

Introduction

Conclusion

SURVIVING TOXIC IN-LAWS

THE BIG BULLIES

MIRIAM DAVIDS

Introduction

The adage has been in existence for ages – "When you marry someone, you do not just marry the individual. Instead, you marry the person's entire family"! 'Entire' would encompass grandparents-in-law, parents-in-law, step-parent-in-laws, ex-spouses, siblings-in-law and their respective families, etc. Your spouse goes through the same experiences, concerning your side of the family.

Apart from having to comprehend their thought processes and behavior, as well as trying to keep everyone happy to the maximum extent possible, there are genuinely embedded familial customs, traditions, and practices to confront too. Naturally, when a whole host of humans are directly or indirectly involved in trying to make your marriage work (in their quirky ways), both of you are bound to feel that 'marriage' must be the biggest challenge of your lives that you have ever faced! Now, all would be well, if there were a few adjustments made from the other side too. However, this does not happen often, and both of you are forced to keep seeking solutions to the frequent 'examination questions' being thrown at you by 'toxic in-laws' throughout your wedded life! Nonetheless, do not despair, for there are ways of handling every situation and converting it to your liking, as this book will show you.

When you are informed, you cannot be deformed. The first thing you should know is this; not all Toxic in-laws are aware that they are toxic. As funny as this sounds, it is true.

Additionally, we shall focus only on parents-in-law or parent-in-law (husband's parents or wife's parents) here. Otherwise, we would need an encyclopedia to cover every kind of relation!

With that in mind, I reached out to friends who have endured severe mistreatment from their in-laws but vowed to fight for their marriage's survival despite seemingly insurmountable opposition.

Sometimes it takes the best things in life to bring the worst out of people. While a statement like that doesn't seem to make sense at first, the stories that follow are a testament to it and the drama that can ensue when families get a little *over*-involved.

For many a little girl, dreams of "Prince Charming" start early. That could be said about Loren Haines. From an early age, she dreamed of wealth and comfort, and to be married to a good man who'd do anything for her. She looked forward to raising children and could already picture a loving husband, a peaceful home, and well-mannered kids surrounding them.

Eventually, Loren would realize the importance of being careful what you wish for.

But, those dreams were starting to come into fruition as Loren came "of age", fell in love with her high school sweetheart named Martin.

Martin was the only son of his parents and had two older sisters. He lost his father early in his teens, but his mom was always there and when Loren came along, adopted her into the family as a child of her own.

Loren was on cloud nine. Martin treated her like a princess and his family loved her; including the sisters, always available for encouragement or a word of advice.

But, that seemed to be short-lived. Dating evolved into an engagement; engagement spurred a wonderful wedding; but once Loren declared, "I do", a switch seemed to go off in Martin's immediate family.

Hardly a month in as newlyweds, Martin's mother became a nightmare. At each opportunity, she'd be hard on Loren, pushing her buttons in hopes she'd react in a way Martin would disapprove of. It seemed as if Martin's mother's goal was to prove Loren wasn't suited to be a wife, let alone a mother.

As it tends to happen, Martin's sisters followed their mother's lead, accusing Loren of messing with Martin's head; trying to keep him from his family. As you might imagine, Loren was dumbfounded. She didn't think of herself as possessive or overbearing at all, and she certainly never interfered with Martin's family issues – including when, immediately after the wedding, his mother moved in.

Soon, insults and sarcasm greeted Loren round each and every corner of her home. She didn't give them much thought at first but soon enough, the pain was unbearable. Loren, being the devoted wife and daughter-in-law, she felt she needed to be, didn't take the bait laid out before her.

In fact, rather than confront his mother or sisters, she took the issue up with Martin; after all, it's his family.

You might imagine the look on Martin's face at hearing of the despicable things his wife is reporting about his mother and sisters.

"Could she really be capable of such nastiness?" Martin wondered. He thought this because he'd never witnessed such behavior from her. His mother was a master of disguise, but soon, she wouldn't try to hide her hatred for Loren.

The complaints kept coming. From Loren's cooking, to her housekeeping; she even accused Loren of breeding harmful microorganisms in the home yet wouldn't return to hers, so the husband and wife could have their lives back. Rather, she told Loren she had every intention of keeping an eye out for her son's wellbeing because he was "married to his ene-my."

Understandably, a tearful Loren shared this with Martin. But when he confronted his mother, she denied. Rather than standing up for his wife, he decided not to pursue a resolution.

Eventually, Martin would lay witness to the sort of mistreatment, ha-tred, and insults his mother was attacking Loren with, yet he remained loyal to his mother.

With this in mind, she became relentlessly overbearing, critical, and antagonizing, making it known that Loren was nowhere near good enough for Martin or their family. She even worked at spreading the word of hatred for Loren to other family members.

Soon, even Martin's sisters, who'd once openly adored Loren, accept-ing her as one of their own, begged their brother to leave her so he could be truly happy. Did I mention Loren had two children in this time? Even so, Martin's mother looked at her more and more with hatred and loathing. Loren felt isolated. Her family was on the west coast, far from being able to intervene and Martin was nowhere near the strong, willful man she thought she'd married.

Nevertheless, Loren persevered. She knew answering hate with hate wasn't going to help the situation at all, so she devised an age-old plan of "killing them with kindness." Anytime Martin's mother complained about her cooking, Loren smiled and gave her other options in the kitchen. Whenever the woman was nasty to her, Loren smiled, said she was "young and ignorant" and promised to do better. When the sisters-in-law would chime in that Loren was far from good enough for Martin, she told them he thought otherwise and that's all that mattered.

What grace? What poise Loren had in dealing with all of this terror?

By this time, Loren had stopped engaging them in arguments and simply ignored them at times; something that seemed to truly bother the mother and sisters, yet they also seemed to back off a bit.

At every opportunity, she greeted her mother-in-law with a smile, and while they never stopped hating Loren, they admired the hell out of her demeanor.

At this point, can you guess how long this treatment has lasted? Your jaw would drop if you heard it was five years. Five years, Loren had dealt with this juvenile and intrusive behavior from her mother and sisters-in-law. It was around here a defining moment came about: Martin was diagnosed with cancer.

While one might think such a severe and dire diagnosis might change a person or an entire family, Martin's mother found it better to blame Loren and her cooking for her son's disease.

It was during one of many regular hospital visits when this came out. While Martin's mother's attitude worsened, Loren's resolve to be kind and loving stayed strong. She'd found out shortly after the diagnosis she was pregnant with their third child. But with the stress of Martin's illness and his mother's relentless hatred abounding, Loren lost the baby.

Again, one might think such a tragedy would warrant a little warmth, love, and care. For many families in turmoil that would be the case; for Martin's mother, it was not.

Her hatred for Loren had never been more evident until one spring morning as Loren entered Martin's hospital room, as she often did. Looking to embrace Martin's mother, she was struck with horror when the woman whispered in her ear, "it should be you lying in this bed."

Still, Loren showed nothing but love. How can a person be so strong? So, resolved? So devoted?

There aren't always happy endings in a situation like this one. Yet, from this point, the story gets a bit brighter. After what seemed like eternities of illness, Martin pulled through chemotherapy and radiation, regaining his strength and receiving a clean bill of health. With a new lease on life, Martin knew what had to be done—something that would be difficult but worth it for his wife and children.

After leaving the care of a hospital, Martin sat down with mom and sisters. "Loren is the one I love and vowed to be with until death," he said. "I'm proud of her for keeping her cool when she could've otherwise reacted to your mistreatment."

Before the conversation was over, he'd asked his mother to hit the road. Before doing so, she maintained her hatred for Loren, but admitted she admired her for the way she carried herself all this time. His sisters echoed the sentiment however cold it still was.

A long overdue apology to Loren had Martin admitting he'd ignored the mistreatment for far too long and promising it would never happen again.

Time would show that Martin would keep his word; not allowing his mother and sisters to visit and overstay their welcome and certainly not allowing them to mistreat Loren.

As for Loren, that dream life she had always wanted was finally started to show itself – five years into her marriage to Martin.

~~

For long-time lovers, Mark and Mable, their future was just about to begin. After years of dating, Mark popped the question in August 2012 with both his and Mable's families present. They were a match made in Heaven; and the engagement was a long time coming for both of their families. Mable was set to be a beautifully elegant bride and seemed to get along wonderfully with all of Mark's family – including his mother and sisters. *"Seemed"* is more than appropriate as she *and* Mark would soon find out.

There always seemed to be a slight tension between Mable and Mark's mother but Mable couldn't figure out exactly what might be causing it. Was she hard to please, Mable often asked herself, but it didn't seem like everyone else felt that way, so she kept her thoughts to herself.

Weeks began to fly by as Mark and Mable began searching for a home together, and of course, started to plan Mable's dream wedding.

The stress started to mount as they both realized there was quite a bit to do in such a short amount of time. The home search seemed to take eternities but eventually, the lovebirds found the perfect spot – just minutes from Mark's work and a couple towns away from his mother.

Excited to share the good news, Mable suggested a family brunch and so the day came for their families to gather and celebrate this monumental step in the pairs' lives.

But, for Mark's mother, no celebration was to be had.

Immediately upon hearing the news, Mable's soon-to-be mother-in-law went on a tirade; throwing a temper tantrum as if she were a child. Spraying vitriol and hatred, she spewed about how far she'd be from her grandchildren. When Mark tried to calm his angry mother, her temper grew worse. Abruptly abandoning the table, Mark, and even his four siblings, sat shocked at the display their mother had just put on.

Even after returning to the table, she muttered under her breath about how all of this was Mable's fault. Mind you, Mable was six-months along with twins, hers and Mark's first children.

"What just happened," Mable asked herself. "How do I get my soon-to-be mother-in-law to understand I'm not taking Mark from her?"

These are just a pair of questions Mable troubled herself within the days and weeks after the brunch – an occasion they'd hoped would've been filled with joy.

Rightfully so, Mark confronted his mother after the disastrous gather, wondering if perhaps it was all just a bit too much for her, causing her reaction. Shortly after the brunch, her stance hadn't changed, so he felt it best to leave her be.

After Mable had moved on from the catastrophic family gathering and continued in wedding planning and preparations, she had an idea. Growing up an only child, she'd always dreamt of a large bridal party. So, she asked Mark's sisters to stand beside her on their special day – an invitation they accepted with joy and honor... at the moment.

Months into planning, Mark's sisters began to take on a bit of an attitude. First, they decided the colors Mark and Mable had chosen didn't work for them. In fact, not only did they demand a change of colors, but a change of dress styles as well. With time running out, rather than honoring the bride's wishes, the trio went above Mable, ordering their own dresses. If that wasn't brash enough, they even called the florist in an attempt to make changes to the arrangements.

Shocked to hear this from her florist, Mable looked to intervene with a meeting of the group. However, the sisters refused to attend or waver in their demands even after a stern talking-to from Mark.

To paraphrase their response, the sisters said if Mark kept them from attending the wedding, they'd find a way to prevent it from happening.

You can only imagine the toll this was all taking on a six-month pregnant bride-to-be. Mable was distraught yet insistent upon not letting her emotions show to the rest of the family. That is, until it all got so much, Mable came down ill.

Hospitalized for nearly two-weeks due to complications with her pregnancy, likely brought on by the immense stress Mark's family had been causing, Mable was eventually discharged and ordered to two-weeks bed rest.

His soon-to-be bride and mother of his twins, Mark became motivated more so than ever to honor Mable's wedding wishes. He saw it as his purpose to lessen the burden on her his family was causing.

Soon, the wedding took place, and appropriately, Mark's sisters apologized for their behavior although the sincerity of it all is still in question.

Just a day before Mark and Mable's twins came into the world, Mark's mother asserted that they'd be living with her, so she could help with the babies. Mable said no! While you might imagine how that went, her mother had already made plans to come to *their* new home to help.

As had become custom, Mark's mother went on a tear, but he put his foot down because it wasn't worth the trouble to please his overbearing mother who was sure to add nothing but stress to Mable's life.

To this day, Mark's mother blames Mable for "changing him" and taking her son away from his family.

~~

Chapter 1: Recognizing Toxic In-Laws

The minute you hear the word, "Toxic," a bottle of poison comes to mind! It is as if your in-laws represent that bottle, which can only bring chaos into your married life! Sometimes, the poisoning is subtle and covert, while at others, it is openly aggressive and confrontational.

At the same time, please note that there is a vast difference between being merely annoying and being highly toxic. The former becomes visible when there are differences of opinion or disagreements about something. However, you tend to forget these annoyances over time, as they do not cause breaches in relationships.

The latter, however, create substantial harm, specifically to your mental health and domestic peace. In fact, it gives them the sadistic pleasure to see how you or your spouse is on the verge of breaking up. You will recognize them by the way they behave.

Smearing your Reputation

The best way to hit back at you for finally recognizing them for what they are is to discredit you in front of your spouse, or even in public. Everything begins with a 'she said' or a 'he said,' wherein the in-laws present themselves as victims of circumstances.

Alternatively, they are willing saints, who are ready to put up with any unkind behavior without complaint. Since they want to stay on top, they do not care if you are humiliated in front of everyone. Repeated gossip, however vicious it might be, does tend to leave its mark. Ultimately, you are painfully surprised to discover that the whole family of 'laws' and 'in-laws' are keen to bully or ostracize you!

It is worse if the smear campaign goes outside the domestic premises. You must be aware of couples, who present themselves in public as charmingly cultured people or beautiful philanthropists, who only want the best for their son/daughter. Well, it is natural for the audience to be impressed! There are subtle insertions of, "I am worried about him/her. After all, I only want him/her to be happy," even into casual conversations. It is a smart way of suggesting that you are not good enough for their son/daughter, or even for their family.

Do not be surprised if the whole community turns against you!

Tactics to Manipulate

People generally deem the mother-in-law, whether it is on the husband's, or wife's side of the family, as the more toxic of the two! As such, this is because she is supposed to come up with innovative tactics to make life miserable for everyone around her!

One such tactic is gaslighting. Here, the mother-in-law aims to undermine your perceptions, such that you begin to second-guess self and even wonder if you are sane! To illustrate, you may decide to confront her about her verbal challenges aimed at you alone, or both of you. Then again, you might ask her why she is trying to sabotage your happily married life via her passive-aggressive behavior. Sometimes, she comes up with things that are not true, but will not accept your corrections.

Whatever is the case, she puts on a pained, shocked, or dull look on her face, and responds with, "I never said that" or "I did not say that at all." To go one step further, she accuses you of being hypersensitive, forcing others to walk on eggshells whenever they are around you. Naturally, when this happens repeatedly, you begin to wonder who is indeed wrong.

After all, how can you tackle someone who flatly refuses to take responsibility for her words or actions, thereby conveying to everyone that you are the one who is confused about everything you say and do! This kind of emotional abuse suffices to destroy your peace of mind and self-confidence over time.

Then again, there is the 'silent' treatment, wherein she 'murders' you in her mind. You have challenged her saintliness, her goodness, etc., and therefore, deserve to be punished. Neither you nor your spouse, exist for her anymore and whatever you say or do no longer matters to her. This kind of silent abuse places her in a position of supreme power but destroys you from within over time.

Particularly, this kind of behavior is torturous, as it stimulates the same part of your brain, which is responsible for informing you about physical pain. You and your spouse may keep apologizing or groveling in front of her as much as you want to, but she will refuse to 'talk.' She takes pleasure in punishing you, for you deserve it!

"I am Always Right"

It is like the parent-child days have returned! Do you remember those days of your childhood, when you had to listen to all the adults around you, for an adult was always right? Well, it is time to recapture those memories now! In-laws are never supposed to be wrong, and you had better accept that without question.

Even if they are wrong, neither one will admit to it. They will never apologize for any errors committed. Then again, if your spouse, whose parents they are, is not taking their side, they decide to punish him/her (as the case may be). They demonstrate open love towards his/her siblings, children, etc., while granting him/her the cold shoulder. We call it 'withholding affection.'

Toxic in-laws are narcissists. They view their children as extensions of their personalities, and not as individuals separate from themselves. As a result, they expect their thought processes, however faulty or narrow-minded they might be, to show up in their offspring. They decide how each of their children must live life, people they should choose as life mates, how they should build their career graphs, etc.

As a result, any deviation from the path chosen for the selected 'child' is a deviation, which needs correcting! It follows, therefore, that you will never be the 'right choice' for their son/daughter. In turn, your choices, words, or even your personal space will receive no respect.

Paradoxically, you must respect everything they say or do, without question! For instance, regardless of your personal or social commitments, you must show up at every family gathering, adapt to their cultural practices and religious traditions, and even give them grandchildren when they expect you to do so! Now, will you strive to please them? Of course, you will, for it does not feel nice to hear grumblings and groanings about how you are neglecting them most of the time!

If anyone of them mentions that, he/she has been ill throughout the week and would have loved to hear from you, will you not feel guilty for failing in that arena? Similarly, if there is a mention of how much they have done for you, and yet, receive so little in return, you are bound to bow under the twin burdens of shame and guilt. Pushing you to take a guilt trip, while they play the roles of victims, is an excellent way of gaining attention!

Then again, do not be surprised if your toxic in-laws, specifically the mother-in-law arrives at your house suddenly without any prior intimation. It is their son's or daughter's home, and they have a right to come whenever they wish to!

Regardless of how unexpected the visit is, you must feel honored and welcome both, or only your mother-in-law with open arms. You must also expect nasty comments on the bad way you have brought up your children, how insignificant your accomplishments are, and so on. You may even assume comparisons between your siblings and self. Whatever matters to her, or to them, in their lives, only hold value.

Blame, Triangulate and Project

Either you or your spouse is to blame for everything that happens. True, all of us 'humans' do take recourse to a blame game, whenever circumstances are not to our liking. However, toxic in-laws tend to carry it to the extreme, even for minor issues, which may be resolved quickly.

According to them, admitting to mistakes or errors is admitting to weakness and deterioration of status. This blame game may remain confined to mere finger pointing or a short emotional outburst, or take dangerous forms, such as calling names, exhibiting a silent rage, or physical violence. Of course, physical aggressiveness is a last resort, when everything else fails. You may attempt to reason with them in many ways, but they will all fail in the face of intense denial or sheer hostility.

When your in-laws resort to triangulation, they are inviting third parties to behave as proxies, negotiators, messengers, etc., in a two-person conflict. You must have seen this happen in dysfunctional families, wherein the male/female parent adopts a divide and rule policy. This individual goes all out to pit his/her children against each other.

As a result, each one competes for his/her attention. Similarly, in this case, the toxic mother-in-law may strive to manipulate her son-in-law or daughter-in-law by dropping subtle hints to her daughter or son. She focuses on finances, housekeeping in general, parenting practices, etc., in such a way that you or your spouse begin to harbor doubts about what is happening within the domestic premises. She even connives to make your spouse or you to feel that all the existing methods are wrong, and it would be best to follow mother-in-law's alternatives. The triangulation method gains higher ground if the in-laws go in for creating alliances that will stand by them always.

Projection refers to transferring your fears, flaws, and wrongdoings onto others. Psychologists call it a defense mechanism. It enables the transferor to condemn others while maintaining his/her superiority at the same time. To illustrate, you are the rude and disrespectful son-in-law or daughter-in-law, according to your in-laws.

Hitherto, do they ever look within themselves, to see if they award even a bit of respect to your spouse or you? Similarly, they may be experts at twisting the truth, but will not hesitate to call you a liar or a dishonest person. You would be foolish to expect them to have any self-awareness or the desire to improve their selves! According to their mindsets, they are perfect, and you should learn from them!

Some toxic in-laws are capable of fooling people easily! They tend to resort to extremely lovely behavior on their 'good' days, compelling you to believe that finally, everything is going to be better. You breathe a big sigh of relief! Then, when you least expect it, they display their wickedly toxic attitude all over again! These are the 'bad' days, which bring you back to the real world with a jolt! They will never change on their own. Do something!

Chapter 2: Dealing with the Controllers

It is easy enough to tell others, including your family members, that you can take charge of your own life, thank you very much! Sometimes, you go a step further and tell them that you would like them to mind their own business and not meddle in your personal life. However, it is somewhat tricky to do the same with 'controlling' in-laws. Additionally, if they comprehend that controlling you or spouse, is the most natural thing in the world, you have had it!

They control because they feel that their son-in-law or daughter-in-law is not capable of looking after self. Therefore, they decide to teach him/her how to handle taxes, shop, cook, look after children, etc. The message is that you, or even both of you, are babies, who do not know what is best for you! At first, you give in, or offer little resistance, believing that if it makes them happy, just let it be! Later on, you begin to protest, gently at first, and louder and louder afterward.

Unfortunately, the results are not going to make you happy, for they will only respond with anger, disdain, or laughter. Over time, you tend to become a nervous wreck. On their part, they have become so psychologically addicted to the habit of control, that, try as they might, they cannot stop their behavior on their own.

In all honesty, they might not even want to, for there is that sense of being powerful, intense and pushy, which gives them great joy. It does not matter what family life is like for you, but it is very comfortable for both of them since they get to do things all their way! As for the destruction of relationships, they really could not care less!

The Covert Controller

All the comments that your in-laws direct at you are rather subtle in nature. Your in-laws are hoping that you will act and behave in the manner that they feel is 'right'. In other words, they are not interested in what you think at all! Regardless, there are ways to deal with these kinds of indirect controllers, especially the more voluble mother-in-law, without losing your cool!

Let us imagine a scenario wherein your mother-in-law is in the kitchen with you (her daughter-in-law), helping you bake some cookies. Somewhere along the line, she is bound to say something. In fact, do not even be surprised if she throws in a comment about the way you are baking them! For instance, she hints that her cookies do not break apart in the middle the way yours do, since she allows them to remain in the oven for just a little while (about three minutes or so) longer.

Now, it should be apparent to even the simplest of mindsets that she is taunting you about your cooking skills! Nonetheless, would it be to your benefit to burst into tears immediately, offer apologies, or fall all over yourself to do it her way? Do not do any of these things! After all, you have baked cookies before, and this is not the first time that you are entering the kitchen.

Similarly, it would not do to go into the confrontational mode by asking your mother-in-law if she was calling you a bad cook. It would not do to suggest that she was implying that you were a bad cook, either. Instead, take a deep breath or two, and offer a calm reply. Ensure that your tone is very casual. You might say, "Oh, when you say this, it seems as if you believe that I am not a very skilled cook."

What do you think will happen next?

There will be a change of subject immediately, as a flustered and embarrassed mother-in-law strives to take control of the situation once again. Alternatively, she may even apologize to you, stating that she never meant it to sound like an insult at all. Whatever is the case, you may rest assured that you will receive no more insults in future! If you want further assurances about the success of this simple technique, wherein you throw the ball into the opposite court and leave it to him/her to react in whatever way he/she wishes to, let us test it on three types of mothers-in-law. Note that they are all indirect insulters.

The first one is the type, who speaks impulsively, and without thinking. This kind of person is bound to be slightly insecure herself, with issues about self-esteem. Additionally, you may not realize it, but she probably feels slightly awed by you. Thanks to her insecurities, she remains continuously irked by people and situations around her. Therefore, even if she notices the tiniest of flaws in the way you make your cookies, she grabs onto it as a weapon to pierce your confidence.

By pointing out your weakness, she strives to distance herself from her own. Alternatively, she may not have been in a great mood at that time and used you as a target to release her internal frustrations. Your tranquil reaction to this heat-of-the-moment woman suffices to point out her rudeness. She has no option but to let you know that she did not mean what she said and that you are not a bad cook at all.

The second category comprises of mothers-in-law, who just cannot resist taking a dig at daughters-in-law! Your mother-in-law believes herself to be a good cook and desires to suggest that you should feel like producing good cookies too. She is subtly stating that her baking skills are better than yours are so that you should feel inferior.

At the same time, she understands she has no right to comment on what you do, and how you do it. However, you will be glad to know that this kind of a person does feel genuinely remorseful after realizing how mean her words sounded to your ears. You may expect an apology or the re-framing of her insult in a more tactful manner. There is a lesson for you here. It is possible to change the behavior of the just-cannot-resist mother-in-law. Whenever she lets, similar abuses fall, begin your reply with, "When you say this, it seems as if you believe" and attach something to it. As she gains greater awareness, her restraint will also increase.

The third kind of mother-in-law, whom everyone refers to as Monster-in-Law, is rather more challenging to tackle. She is keen to break up your relationship with your spouse, as well as destroy your self-confidence as severely as possible. Unlike the other types of mothers-in-law, she will not give in so effortlessly.

In fact, she refuses to expose herself in front of you. Therefore, she will simply change the subject and move on to something mundane. Nevertheless, do not give up. Continue to retaliate with the same sentence every time she launches a new attack on your self-esteem. Over time, when she realizes that your balloon of self-confidence refuses to be punctured, she will abandon her strategy!

Outlined below are a few more examples to ensure that you get the hang of how to reply to caustic tongues.

To illustrate, your mother-in-law comments upon your 'casual' look for attending a nighttime social event. Express the thought that it seems as if she believes that you do not know how to dress appropriately for social affairs.

What do you think will happen next?

If this comment is from the insecure mother-in-law, she will agree that you do not deserve this kind of condescension. She will tell herself that it is her insecurity coming in the way of your bonding with her.

If this is the type of woman, who dearly wishes you to look as pleasant as she does, she will regret her rudeness. She was trying to tell you something but had not been very tactful in doing so.

If this is from the Monster-in-Law, she will merely divert the conversation into another direction.

Thus, get into the mode of – "When you say this, it seems as if you believe that

- I am not an intelligent individual
- I am incompetent in handling household finances
- I am not properly raising my children, etc."

Are fathers-in-law any less caustic? No, they definitely are not!

For instance, a father-in-law may suggest to his son-in-law that money does not seem to matter much in his life, considering the type of jobs he has been selecting thus far. The son-in-law must come back with an intelligent and calm reply, "When you say this, it seems as if you believe that my profession/job is not worthy enough of meeting your high standards." Taken aback, a flustered father-in-law will apologize for his rudeness, suggest that he did not mean for his comment to sound that way, or change the subject!

Similarly, he may taunt the son-in-law about raising children in a somewhat liberal manner. The response should end with, 'incapable of disciplining my kids.' Throw the ball back into his court and wait!

The Overt Controller

Some people prefer to exert direct control, believing that it is their birthright to do so. They could not care less if they are playing by the rules or not! They want to order and command, expecting you to follow whatever they say. For instance, your tough-minded in-laws take pleasure in pointing out that you are doing everything wrong, whenever you refuse to do it 'their way.'

Again, go back to being calm and restrained. "When you say this, it seems as if you believe that I should do everything your way only and never my way." Your casual retort will fetch positive results, as their insults lose power!

Take care not to use this sentence with the covert controllers, for it will result in open war!

The Controller who goes to Extremes

These toxic in-laws take every decision right out of your hands! They refuse to use verbalizations. To them, direct actions are more important. To illustrate, they may have set up an appointment with the hairdresser to have their son's haircut, without even bothering to ask him. The excuse is that his hair is beginning to look very shaggy or unruly. It would be good for the son to reply calmly, "It seems like you have decided on my behalf that I should have a haircut." Will they have the grace to look ashamed? Of course, they will!

Therefore, whenever they meddle too much in your affairs and personal decisions, both of you (husband and wife) must go in for calm replies that begin with, "I see that you have decided for me..." and attach a sentence focusing on the decision they made on your behalf. It may relate to buying a birthday present, handing over a new car to a teenaged grandchild holding a driving license in his hand, deciding which restaurant you must visit on your birthday, etc.

On a final note, if you are feeling quite overwhelmed at how much you must remember, just make a list of potential insults and your reply to each one. After all, you know your toxic in-laws for what they are, as you have been in touch with them ever since you got married! In fact, you may even memorize your attachments, so that you are always prepared.

Alternatively, you may go in for a simple accessory that is suitable for every occasion and every controlling behavior. "When you say this, it seems as if you believe that I have done something wrong." Whatever method you opt for, do not ever use derogatory language to describe yourself. For instance, you are not a slob, a jerk, an idiot, a bum, etc. Do remember that you must respect yourself if you want others to respect you. Above all, your spouse and you must stand together, if you wish to have domestic harmony.

Chapter 3: Handling the Critics, Manipulators and Narcissists

They Criticize Everything

They are the perfect stereotype of what toxic in-laws are all about! They take strong exceptions to everything that your spouse and you do. It could relate to dress choices, lifestyles, parenting practices, career options, religious beliefs, entertainment choices, etc. They do not mind making their disapproval loud and clear, whether it is to your faces or others outside the house. Such vicious personal attacks often tend to throw you so much out of balance that you wish the ground would open up and swallow you!

The critics do not care that you and your spouse have been striving to do everything right in every way possible. They do not mind stepping over the invisible boundaries that you have drawn and intruding into your private space. They refuse to believe that they are hurtful, inappropriate and offensive in their verbalizations and actions.

In fact, they express amazement at your objections to them behaving like good teachers for children who seem to have gone awry. Whatever is the case, it is high time that you develop some strategies, to save your marriage.

1. Declare your Authority

True, your parents or parents-in-law are older, and you will always remain a 'child' to them. However, you have grown up now and are quite capable of taking your own decisions. You have the right to handle things the way you want to, regardless of whether your actions appeal to others or not. It does not even matter if you make mistakes.

You will learn from them and do better next time. Therefore, make it very clear that you and your spouse are the authority figures in your family. You will always respect your elders. In turn, they must respect your family's wishes too.

2. Put them in their Places

No, this is not as rude as it sounds! It means that your toxic in-laws must recognize their limits and remain within them. For instance, it is quite common to find toxic in-laws going overboard with their criticism of your childrearing practices. You need not get into direct conflict with them over this matter but just issue a mental challenge. You may suggest as calmly as possible, "You are not criticizing our way of rearing children again, are you?" Of course, they are bound to become defensive and react the first time firmly.

However, if you keep repeating it, there is bound to come a time when they feel powerless to respond. You will have to try and try again if you desire to change their attitude towards your family and you.

In case, your patient responses fetch no results; you will have to change your tactics. You will have to let them know clearly, how their behavior is making you feel. Issue a firm warning that if they continue to cross the borderline, there will be significant consequences in the offing.

3. Refuse to Move an Inch

You have heard the saying that if you give a person an inch, he tries to grab a yard! Therefore, do not go all soft and mushy, when recriminations and tears come your way. You will have to stand your ground, wherein your in-laws must consider changing their ways to suit you, and not the other way around!

To illustrate, overly devout in-laws may demand that you attend lengthy morning services in church every Sunday. This is because they feel that they are more spiritually rewarding than the short services conducted during weekdays. However, you prefer to go occasionally, whenever you get time, since you are busy, working professionals.

This constant bugging can irritate you no end, especially when snide comments about lack of faith in God, imperfect spiritual practices, etc., accompany it too. Nonetheless, it is your life. Your soul and its safety also lie within your own hands. No one else needs to bother about it. Therefore, do not budge an inch, for if you give in now, you will keep giving in always. Do what you feel is right.

4. Maintain a Distance

It would be good to keep a geographical distance between your toxic in-laws and your family, even if you have to relocate. You may no longer be able to visit them on foot but will need to drive a reasonable distance instead! Then again, your spouse (husband/wife) should not expect you to spend time with his/her parents when he/she is not around. Similarly, whenever any unpleasant issues crop up, he/she should be ready to tackle them.

In case, occasional or monthly visits are necessary, for maintaining a bond with your toxic in-laws, you might suggest neutral territories as the best places for your family gatherings. A public restaurant, for instance, will not permit them to be in charge. Additionally, you will feel more in charge of the situation, as you are not a guest at their house.

5. Do not Give or Receive Financial Support

Money is one of the leading culprits for breaking or harming relationships. Considering, that, your in-laws possess a dangerous mindset, you would be doing yourself more harm than good by accepting financial support or even expensive gifts readily.

Note that every kind of support comes with a string attached to it. Ask yourself if you would like to owe anything to this couple, now or in the future. At the same time, refuse to grant any support to your in-laws. They will feel obliged to help you with wise advice in return for your monetary help or gifts. You are better off without this advice!

6. Re-Draw the Boundaries

Sometimes, your energy just drains away as you struggle to cope with the same issue repeatedly. It drains away, if new problems join the old too. For instance, your toxic in-laws may take sadistic pleasure in bestowing unwanted gifts on every birthday and festive event. This gesture is a subtle reminder that you should be doing the same too. The first step towards resolution would be to have a frank talk with your in-laws about the whole thing and suggest that no more gifting take place.

However, if they refuse to listen or exhibit no reaction at all, you will need to offer a firm suggestion that there would be no more exchange of presents at any time of the year. You are setting this boundary for the good of all. Alternatively, you might hint that whatever gifts came your way, you would merely donate them to charity.

7. Tackle your Spouse

Yes, you will have to do this too, if you feel that he/she is not handling the situation correctly! There is no denying that even an overly 'grown-up' child will feel bad about allotting negative labels to a parent. He/she will even feel remorseful about betraying parental love. Then again, there is the torture of having to take sides concerning expressing viewpoints, assigning blame, or showing support.

Therefore, it is imperative that you provide assurances of standing with him/her all the way, wherein it will not feel like he/she is disloyal to his/her parents.

Also, you will not come in the way of his/her maintaining a good bonding with his/her parents. You want to seek some respect for both of you and your wishes. After all, you owe it to each other to make your marriage work, without letting hard feelings and negative energies coming in the way. You mean a lot to each other, and your 'own' family means a lot to both of you!

Whether he/she likes it or not, it is imperative that your spouse deals with the problem directly and stand firm in his/her resolve. It is crucial that he/she have frank discussions with toxic in-laws and let them know that he/she has a life of his/her own now.

They Love to Manipulate

These toxic in-laws may seem similar to controllers but are not. They use your spouse or you as tools to gain whatever they want. If it were your parents, they would love to spend time with you. If it were your spouse's parents, they would like to spend time with him/her. Then again, they are eager to gain recognition from their grandchildren, peers, etc. To do this, they will take recourse to any and every method possible.

The approaches include bribery, tantrums, playing on feelings of guilt, etc. Your emotions, choices, and thoughts are not important at all. They feel that they deserve 'something' and go all out to obtain it!

You might understand better by perusing the example outlined below.

You are a happily married couple with a child. While your husband is a European, you are an American. Both of you are working professionals, and therefore take joint responsibility for handling all manner of chores inside and outside the house. Your parents live elsewhere, while your divorced in-laws live in the same city as you do. Naturally, your in-laws keep visiting you, or you keep going over to their separate houses.

Overall, you get along famously with your father-in-law. However, specific cultural differences do intrude at times into your relationship, thereby creating tension. As such, this is because you find him highly traditional in contrast to your liberal mindset. Moreover, when he visits, his word must be law.

To illustrate, you cannot decide what the menus for meals must be, when you should eat, etc. In case, you refuse to fall in with his plans; he tends to become offended. Your husband prefers to remain a quiet observer, rather than help you out in handling such situations.

Your mother-in-law is quite a virulent character, as evinced by the attacks she launches against your child-rearing practices. She does not mind how she castigates you, whether in private or in front of your spouse. The last straw is when she initiates a verbal tirade against you in front of everyone when you have invited members of both sides of the family to a Christmas dinner.

According to her, you have no concern for your spouse at all. You are ill-treating him. It is thanks to you that he is looking so thin and worn out. Additionally, you are burdening him with too much of housework, which is all wrong. The entire audience is left stunned and dazed, especially your parents, by what is happening at a happy family gathering.

How will you and your husband react?

You are apparently too shocked to rush into any speech. Your spouse agrees that his mother was entirely out of line with her and decides to keep a distance from her for some time at least. At the same time, he cannot forget that she is his mother after all and keeps insisting that she did not mean what she was saying. Therefore, you give in and continue to stay in touch with her. She does come over to your place occasionally, but things are no longer the same between her and you. You would only like your children to keep in touch with their grandmother and her culture. It is natural that since she did not feel the need to apologize for her actions, you decide to maintain a cool distance from her.

Lately, though, both the in-laws have begun to utilize manipulative tactics while visiting you. Of course, each of them does come to interact with the grandchildren. However, they have also started to spend more and more time with your husband. It is as if he is a toddler all over again, and they are the adoring parents! You do understand and do not interfere, for they had to undergo several trials and tribulations while rearing him.

However, it is too much to expect that you will allow them to take over the entire house in the name of adoring parents, while they are here! What is more annoying is the way your mother-in-law clings to your husband, hugging and kissing him all the while, while ignoring your kids. Your husband does not seem to mind giving in to their every wish and fancy, refusing to stand up to them or the deterioration in familial relationships. It escapes his eye that your toxic in-laws are trying to manipulate him to leave you and the children.

Well, now, what is the solution to handling such manipulative toxic in-laws?

As mentioned earlier, the family had faced difficult circumstances during your husband's childhood. It also necessitated a period of separation between parents and son. Realizing this, your husband is feeling guilty about the whole thing.

He knows that his parents had a difficult time bringing him up, and therefore, he should feel immensely grateful to them. Your toxic in-laws have witnessed and comprehended this 'guilt' and going all out to exploit it to their advantage. Your husband feels that he owes them all the time he can in the form of compensation.

As a result, he refuses to stand united with you. Then again, standing up to a parent may have resulted in unpleasant consequences in the past. The divorce between the in-laws has not helped either.

At the same time, you cannot remain a mute bystander. Therefore, as soon as you get the chance, you must initiate a discussion with your husband, when the toxic in-laws and the children are not around. You may even go out to a secluded place to have your 'talk.'

Focus on how he changes when his parents are around, what happens to him when they visit, how you can bring back familial bonding amongst all of you, etc. be calm and reasonable, while all the while inserting subtle suggestions about setting reasonable boundaries and how much flexibility you may award your in-laws.

It is imperative that both of you come up with strategies that bring about positive changes in the situation. Please note that he may not understand your need for back up immediately. You will have to work on his mindset and make him see things with an objective eye.

Stress that it is essential for you to stay with each other and not turn against each other, for you are as important to your children, as his parents are to him.

Have realistic expectations about your in-laws. It is too late to change them completely. However, you may promise yourself to bring about modifications in your behavior and reactions. For instance, your mother-in-law feels that your child-rearing practices are not good.

Fine, ask her how she fed her children, whether her husband helped her with the housework or not, etc. Who knows, the two of you may yet become good friends! Comfort yourself with the fact that she is a bitter person from within. Therefore, she does not actually direct it at you. She is storing more and more within herself. Repeat this to yourself several times. You should be all right!

Handling Narcissists

You cannot believe it when you see your toxic in-laws for the first time when your would-be life partner takes you to meet them! They are so amazingly charming and friendly that you feel that all the talk circulating in the neighborhood about this family must be a mere exaggeration and nothing more. In fact, you just cannot wait to enter this supposedly narcissistic family! Of course, when reality finally strikes, you will find it difficult to weather the blows!

1. Prior to the Engagement

Mere meetings are not sufficient to unsettle toxic in-laws. After all, everybody goes in for casual dating. Furthermore, their son/daughter believes in the tell-all philosophy, as firmly as they do. The time is also ripe for squashing rumors about something going on between their beloved child and potential spouse.

Instead, they take sadistic glee in countering the gossip with untruths about you. To go one step further, they even invite previous 'dates' or 'partners' to hobnob with their beloved 'child,' and see if the partnership can progress towards a wedding. These previous dates are easy to manipulate, unlike you. Thus, they go back to their complacent mood, confident that their son/daughter will never do anything without consulting them first.

As soon as their son/daughter announces that an engagement is in the offing, however, there is a call for battle! You are highly unsuitable and inadequate for both, their child and the family. Their son/daughter can never be happy with you.

If this is not enough, the narcissistic and toxic in-laws get to work on your mindset. There are subtle hints that you must remain under their control, refuse to set boundaries, etc., if you wish to enter this family.

Everything takes place in the presence of their son/daughter, albeit so covertly that he/she does not have an inkling of how severely they are threatening you. There is even a hint of not attending the engagement, or also supporting it if you refuse to adhere to the in-love-with-themselves couple's requirements. The idea behind all this drama is to ensure that you break your engagement with your would-be spouse. Nonetheless, do not give in tamely. If you are sure that this is the right person for you, cling on!

2. Time for a Wedding

Since the toxic in-laws could not stop, the engagement from going through, they will play their next shot on the wedding day. If you had been harboring the notion that these narcissists would remain quiet in public, you were wrong! There are bound to be loud laments about seating arrangements being inappropriate, for instance.

Then again, they will not refrain from passing snide remarks about the wedding attire of the spouse-to-be. It is supposed to be lacking in style and color.

If they do not get the opportunity to occupy center stage, you may expect the narcissists to convey their unhappiness through words like victimized, improper, and so on. True, it is your day. However, your toxic in-laws feel that it should be theirs and theirs alone. They want the audience to remember their words and actions, and not the wedding ceremony.

By doing this, it does their oversized egos a great lot of good! It does not matter if the onlookers feel disgusted, amazed, etc. If this were not all, they would like to occupy the stage at the reception ceremony too, and in fact, at every event involving both of you!

Both of you may go all out to appease them. It will do no good. Therefore, you might as well grit your teeth and go through the ceremony first, while promising yourself that you will take care of these matters later.

3. Post Marriage

If you believe that the intense drama that preceded both, your engagement and wedding, is over, you are over-optimistic! Your narcissistic and toxic in-laws are keen to continue the game, albeit in a subtler manner. After all, they believe that they are the best in the entire 'human' kingdom!

Additionally, if they were to choose someone for their son/daughter, they would have found someone truly worthy of their family. Do not be surprised by the lewd jokes and sarcastic comments that they direct at you as if they are throwing darts at your body. They love being bigots, exhibiting prejudices against your cultural practices, religious beliefs, etc.

As per their opinion, you are in a lower socioeconomic class from them. Therefore, you may not join their family discussions. Even if you do, you will experience isolation, as the toxic in-laws focus on people and stories from the past.

Since you were not part of this family's history, you feel like an uninvited outsider. As such, this is the narcissists' way of demonstrating that you can never 'fit' into this exalted family. Do not expect your spouse to comprehend your feelings. According to him/her, these comments are harmless, and you are overreacting to the situation.

Do not argue with him/her in front of his/her parents. They will be thrilled to witness the wedge they have driven into your marriage via their wiles. Additionally, you do not want your spouse to begin believing that his/her partner is crazy!

4. Recognizing the Signs and Symptoms of Narcissists

You will realize that you have entered a narcissist's family when you observe these signs.

- Your spouse's parents keep calling up, not once in a day/week, but several times every day.

- They drop in without warning, several times in a week.

- Your spouse does not mind, for he/she feels guilty if not in regular touch with his/her narcissistic parents.

- At the same time, there is frustration, uneasiness, and annoyance at the control that his/her parents exert over him/her.

- He/she does not have a life of his/her own.

- Keeping in touch deprives you too, of 'your' time with your spouse.

- However, if you ever try to criticize this overly involvement of your parents-in-law in your spouse's life, you will be heading towards a heated altercation.

- In fact, your spouse will find all kinds of excuses for his/her parents' behavior.

- Regarding yourself, either your toxic in-laws reject/isolate you, or go out of the way to be friendly whenever your partner is complaining about you.

You may not be aware of it, but narcissists are highly concerned about control and self-image. Based upon whatever is at stake, your in-laws will vacillate between expressing disapproval/approval. Their behavior is also dependent upon the kind of audience observing it. Thirdly, they would like to know if their behavior would bring them benefits or not.

To illustrate, they might praise you to the skies in public, but bash your head into the ground in private! Another kind of narcissist couple would like an assurance from you, whether overt or covert, that they may remain in control over your spouse, without your interference.

Should you object, be prepared for verbal assaults or exhibition of immense rage. Alternatively, they may promise to see that your spouse withholds his/her attention, money, or love from you. Thus, they desire to maintain a healthy public image and power over your spouse in private.

What strategies can you adopt to resolve your marital issues?

To begin with, do not just take everything lying down. The first opportunity you get, request your spouse to spare some time for a discussion. You must voice your concerns gently, firmly and clearly, without putting the other person's back up.

Let your spouse know that you are not complaining but do have some expectations from your marriage. It can only work if there is frank and earnest communication between you. If your spouse understands how his/her parents' behavior is destroying your marriage, he/she may decide to communicate with his narcissistic family.

If he/she succeeds in assuring the toxic in-laws that he/she will never isolate them, despite having a partner at home, it should do the trick. The parents should realize that it is possible to 'share' this individual with his/her spouse without becoming paranoid about it.

Then again, it would be a good idea for your spouse and you to set boundaries regarding back and forth visits, such that each couple retains its privacy. Both of you must put up a united front before your toxic in-laws, regardless of your private struggles and personal hang-ups.

Only then, will the narcissists leave you alone! Make sure that your spouse understands your intense need for protection, not only for now but also throughout your wedded life. It is imperative that he/she stands by your side and rushes to your defense whenever your toxic in-laws insult you. If this does not happen, your toxic in-laws will feel overjoyed to discover that they had been right all along!

Similarly, request an outsider to assist you in comprehending narcissism and the strategies to deal with it. Ensure that this person is not a family member, but someone with professional expertise. You need not harbor worries about betraying the trust of your spouse or in-laws, for you are only trying to rectify a highly intolerable situation via safe methods. This counselor should be able to prevent a nervous breakdown!

Chapter 4: Tackling Miscellaneous Issues

Apart from the above, you may come across other types of toxic in-laws.

She Engulfs Him

Rarely, does the father go in for this kind of a tactic to retain control over his children. It is the mother's prerogative to behave as if her children have never left the family nest. Wherever they are, she will reach out to 'live through them,' thereby causing intense misery to the newcomer who hooks up with one of her children as a life partner.

Generally, she loves to 'engulf' a much-loved son, regardless of whether she is making him happy/unhappy. He must remain attached to her apron strings forever, allowing his family to take second place. Towards this end, she will strive to be at his side always and be part of everything that he does or undertakes. It does not matter in the least, whether her behavior is appropriate, or even particularly helpful. In short, this toxic mother-in-law is the master puppeteer, who runs the show, and anyone who dares to come in her way had better beware!

It is hard for you, who have entered the arena of marriage with starry dreams in your eyes, to comprehend why the mother, who declares that she wants her son to be happy, smothers him to such an extent that his entire personality becomes stunted. She does not even realize that she is invading the fabric of his life to such an extent, that it can only tear and tatter.

On his part, the son does not even strive to break free of the leash that holds him back so tightly. He is grown up, yet incapable of thinking for himself. He is always bowing to emotional blackmail, engaged in a relentless tug-of-war with his mother, or setting out on a guilt trip.

Maybe, his parents have drilled into his mind that he is duty bound to care for them until the end of their lives. Well, this is entirely correct, but is it right to expect him to kill all his ambitions, desires, etc., along the way? Whatever the reasons may be, he is the victim of an 'engulfer'!

In a way, it is not his fault, for his mother placed him in a unique mold and sculpted him in alignment with her desires, right from birth. Therefore, Mama's boy has grown into Mama's man, destined to obey commands, fear to revolt, and give in to emotional blackmail and scheming without protest.

As a result, his dreams, aspirations, etc., remain tucked away in dark corners, never to seen again. Your mother-in-law loves to boast about her ever-dutiful son to anyone and everyone who cares to listen.

However, she omits to mention the strategies she uses to get him to obey, such as maintaining deadly silence, offering the cold shoulder, engaging in emotional dramas, cribbing loudly all the time, going on hunger strikes and giving vent to sorrowful complaints. She has bestowed so much love and attention upon him during his growing years, and he must do the same now.

Naturally, you cannot expect any support from such a man, even if you remain married to him for the rest of his life. Therefore, the only thing you can do is to put as much distance between your toxic mother-in-law and self.

You may have to walk out of the marriage because your spouse is never going to put a marital relationship above the relationship with his mother. On your part, you will become a nervous wreck, trying to fulfill unjust demands, seek approval, etc., if you continue to stay on. True, his parents are irreplaceable. At the same time, you cannot destroy your life and happiness. Therefore, put an end to everything, seek financial independence and carry on with living.

Cutting the Apron Strings

Many married couples invite trouble into their lives, thanks to permitting toxic in-laws to interfere too heavily in their lives. For instance, instead of asking you to share in decision-making, your spouse may decide to rely heavily on his/her parents to present their viewpoints.

Then again, your spouse may feel that his/her parents will fulfill his/her emotional needs, and not you. In a third scenario, one of you spills the beans about every marital conflict that takes place, to your parents. By doing this, it can make the other partner to feel terribly bad about the invasion of privacy.

How will this affect your marital life?

1. Inability to Engage in Healthy Decision Making

Your toxic in-laws received the right to make their own decisions when they embarked upon their wedded life. Well, they should award the same freedom to their grown-up children too. Of course, there are parents-in-law, who refuse to interfere unless asked to do so.

However, you are dealing with toxic in-laws here! They are noticeably too fond of offering 'wisdom,' whether it may be solicited or not. They feel that they are showing you how deeply they are concerned about your spouse and you. Nevertheless, you are not willing to thank them for it, for you feel that they do not respect or trust you.

Additionally, the fact that your spouse is incapable of taking independent or joint decisions, without dragging in-laws into the picture, irritates you! What your spouse does not realize is that by running to parents for advice on everything connected to his/her life, he/she is leaving the door wide open for them to walk in anytime they please. Soon enough, you should find them intruding in every aspect of your life, as well as correcting decisions that you have already made.

Now, you cannot let this carry on forever, especially if it is going to result in heated marital conflicts. Therefore, ask your spouse to sit down with you and have a discussion. However, be diplomatic and subtle in pointing out how your spouse's behavior is threatening your peace of mind. State that you do comprehend that your in-laws have exhibited a lot of goodwill towards your marriage and family.

However, autonomy works better at times. Towards this end, therefore, come up with a strategy that appeals to all, and hurts none. For instance, you could make some personal decisions about your family alone, by yourselves. In case, there were significant decisions to make, which would benefit via the inputs of experienced people, you could consult both sets of parents or just one set.

In case, things do not work out even after your discussion, because your toxic in-laws persist in their interfering practices, seek a consultation with a marriage counselor. You must set some boundary lines!

2. Inability to Destroy the Emotional Apron Strings

Now, it is not nice that your spouse prefers to fulfill his/her emotional needs through the relationship he has with his/her parents. Nevertheless, this is akin to betraying your faith in him/her.

However, why does this happen?

If you are a wife, you may feel that your husband has no interest in what you did the whole day at home, or at work. You would like to discuss your experiences during the day with him, but he prefers not to be bothered. Frustration can lead you to your parents, wherein you pour out your heart to them.

Alternatively, you may be the husband, who is frustrated because your spouse shows no interest in your work or thought processes. Instead, she seems to have better bonding with the kitchen, TV, etc. What will you do then? You will begin a long conversation with your mother and tell her about your day. Naturally, your spouse is going to feel highly ignored.

This just will not do, for the 'frustrated spouse is handing over the reins of control to toxic in-laws. They could be on either side of the family. Additionally, both of you are losing respect for each other. That respect will deteriorate further, as parents-in-law decide that they must take over the roles of supporters of their son/daughter.

Therefore, take constructive steps to resolve the situation before it is too late. For instance, you might tell your parent/parents that you would like to limit your conversations to about once a week, instead of daily. You could also put in a casual word about adhering to general topics, instead of the personal or familial.

Alternatively, you may decide to change the course of your conversations on your own. Unless your parent/parents ask about it, do not mention certain things, or even give explanations. For instance, keep discussions related to life's goals, unexpected financial situations, etc., limited to husband and wife only. Note that active emotional bonding builds up healthy intimacy in marriage.

At the same time, despite your in-laws being toxic in behavior, do not request your spouse to sever all relations with them. Ensure that there is a good adjustment, such that there is time to nurture every relationship within the family. Your spouse, in turn, must suggest the same for your parents.

3. Over Sharing of Confidential Matters

Your toxic in-laws, whether from the husband's side or the wife's side, are bound to be overjoyed every time they hear a story of a tremendous marital fight! Whenever you and your spouse engage in a war, both of you rush to your particular cell phones or go in person to your parents' house to discuss all the gory details. Alternatively, just one of you may have this habit of betraying the other partner's trust. Whatever is the case, this kind of behavior is an assured way of destroying a marriage.

If neither of you shows respect towards one another, how do you expect your respective parents to have healthy relationships with your spouse or you? You may argue that you do reconcile within a few hours after the fight, or maybe after a couple of days or so.

What you forget is that your family members do not know that. They will only store memories of your outpourings in their brain and bring it up each time another unpleasant incident takes place. It is as if the new event is a follow up of the last one.

Above all, your spouse's parents will always harbor suspicions about you, while your parents do the same as far as your spouse is concerned.

It is not wise to request parents or parents-in-law to act as referees for your verbal tennis matches. Do remember that they have brought up your spouse or you. Therefore, it is hard for them to be objective about anything, especially if they have always wondered if their son/daughter is good enough for you! It would be nice on their part to send you home and suggest that you work it out amongst yourselves. However, do you believe that toxic in-laws will engage in such mature behavior?

The worst scenario is when your verbal conflict turns into a physical one! Whichever is the injured party or the victim, must seek safety immediately. At such a time, sensible parents may suggest viable solutions to repair your marriage. Toxic in-laws will straightaway recommend a separation, probably even a legal one!

In general, how can you deal with this issue of refusing to sever the apron strings?

- Begin with the idea that you are a team, wherein your commitment to each other is so strong that you can work through any problem successfully.

- Strive to come up with strategies to fulfill each other's needs without involving parents or in-laws.

- Place limits on how many parent-child conversations you may take in a week or a month.

- Neither of you should engage in open criticism of your in-laws, however toxic they may be.

- Note that you and your spouse know much more about your parents than the other one does.

- Initiate discussions when both of you have fed well, feel good and are well rested. Tired minds cannot comprehend everything well.

- In case, you need to inform/confront your parents or parents-in-law, the 'own' child must take over. It is high time they understood that their child is a grown-up adult now, and capable of handling life on his/her own.

- If the parents cannot handle the conversation, do not worry. They should be able to come around to your point of view sometime or the other.

- Above all, vow to stand by each other throughout your married life, especially if toxic in-laws prove too meddlesome and are eager to destroy your happiness.

- Take a stand if your in-laws demean your wife/husband in your presence, or counter her/his authority. Send across the message that you do love your parents, but your partner is equally important in your life too.

In case, you and your spouse reach an impasse about cleaving the apron strings, consult a professional.

Ignoring Boundaries

No relationship can sustain in the absence of a healthy boundary or fencing. However, toxic in-laws refuse to look at boundary lines. In fact, they do not prove deterrents to whatever their minds have set out to do. For instance, both, your spouse and you would like them to inform you of their coming.

They will walk in unannounced whenever they please, believing that they have the right to visit whenever they wish. It does not matter to them that their grown-up child deserves a life of his/her own. They will still monitor him/her regularly.

They will even demand that your spouse and you share special news with them! Worst of all, you may say goodbye to privacy, since news about personal happenings and personal business are spread all over town!

The only way to handle them is for your spouse and you to talk to them firmly and reset your boundaries. Let them know that you will not tolerate unnecessary interference in your life.

Relying too Much on a Grown-up Child

Oh, these toxic in-laws will cling and cling, whatever anyone might say! They have grown so used to depending on your spouse that they are helpless if left on their own. True, they can still learn to look after themselves, individually with so many caregivers around.

Nonetheless, they prefer to play the roles of king and queen in distress all the time! It is worse if only one in-law is there. The other one may have departed to his/her Heavenly abode or walked out of the marriage.

Naturally, the remaining in-law believes that only her 'child' can ensure that she is left emotionally satisfied. This in-law even believes that your spouse and you will benefit. You will receive immense love in return for proving useful! Should the relied-upon child place his/her life partner's needs first, recriminations, bitter outbursts, etc., follow. This kind of behavior can play havoc with both, your marital, as well as your familial life.

There is no instant solution for this kind of problem. You will have to strive to make these 'dependent' parents 'independent.' If you must take a drastic step like moving away, do so and of course, do not be so cruel that you cut off all contact. Ensure that they have whatever they need but can still take care of many things on their own. Above all, keep in touch by going over to their place sometimes, and inviting them over, at others.

Addicted to Something?

Sometimes, a parent-in-law, or even both in-laws, may be addicted to illicit substances, cigarettes, or alcohol. Considering, that, your in-laws already possess a toxic mindset, this kind of toxicity on top of it, can prove unnerving. You and your spouse will need to be at their disposal, for you never know what will happen next. It could be that other siblings do not care, or do not exist. Therefore, you have to face the burden of looking after their needs all by yourselves.

All your plans for arranging family get-togethers or outings revolve around how the addicted person will behave next! Then again, you must be on a 24 x 7 standby, since health issues can strike anytime. Since you never expected this to happen when you first got married, it can place an enormous strain on marital happiness.

Sit with your spouse and work out how best you can give the best to your kids and yourselves, without upsetting your in-laws. You might even find out about reliable de-addiction centers and get the addicted in-law admitted at one of them.

The Gas Lighters

As mentioned earlier, your toxic in-laws will deny everything that they have uttered, while coming up with their versions of what happened. They have mastered the art of lying and are good weavers of stories. However, they will make it seem as if you are the one who is doing all the lying, thanks to your eternally confused mindset!

As they continue to fill your mind with doubts about what you said and did, you gradually begin to wonder if you are going insane! It is a kind of pleasurable game with them, to see you be at odds with yourself. Worst of all, even your spouse will begin to lose trust in you. Take care that you do not reach the stage where he/she suggests medical treatment.

There is nothing to do, but to find ways to counter their every move in the most intelligent way possible. Refuse to let them push a wedge into your happily married life.

Conclusion

It appears as if the harmful materials present in the environment or the laboratory, are less detrimental, as compared to living and breathing toxic in-laws! Regardless of whatever form they take, toxic in-laws are interested in only one thing, which is, self-centered and selfish survival at the cost of their child's or child's partner's happiness. Towards this end, they will do anything and everything. Therefore, it is up to your spouse and you to counter their evil actions with your wits about you, especially if you want your marriage to survive against all the odds. Whatever happens, if you and your spouse stand united, you should be able to beat them at their own games!

Wish you all the best!

~~

You've heard the age-old expression of things not mixing well like oil and water a thousand times, but how many times have you attributed that adage to marriage and family life. Let's get real. We're not talking about *any* marriage and family life; we're talking about the relationship between a mother-in-law and her son's marriage. That's when things can really get messy!

Such is the case with Greg and Nancy.

Married young, the two often tried at having children. It was a dream for both of them. But that dream was beginning to fade as Nancy would have numerous miscarriages, losing child after child.

Absolutely heartbroken, it seemed as if this dream might never come true. One might imagine the emotional toll such loss could have on their families as well. It's during times like these; families are expected to join together for the healing process, lifting up their loved ones and caring for them in their time of need.

But, Greg's mom wanted no part of that. In fact, it became clear the woman was hell-bent on blaming Nancy, especially after losing their second child.

"What would make her think these things?" Nancy wondered to herself.

She'd on many occasions expressed to Greg how she wondered if she'd *ever* be fortunate enough to have grandchildren; all the while blaming Nancy for the miscarriages.

In all, Nancy would lose four children to miscarriage and not receive an ounce of sympathy from her cold, wretched, witch of a mother-in-law. It would later be revealed that blaming Nancy for losing children was one of the more tame things she was capable of.

Through years of marriage and attempts at pregnancy, the grief of loss was piling up for Nancy. After the third miscarriage, and Greg's mother's accusations, Nancy couldn't help by being overcome by emotions all the time. She was missing work and had fallen into a deep, deep depression. Greg, who'd seemed to be supportive through it all, was beginning to turn on her as well, chiming in with his mother's comments on blame.

After Nancy's fourth miscarriage, her mother-in-law became unrecognizable. Tension continued to build, and she made it no secret that she hated the woman her son had married.

She'd overheard her say, "I warned you about Nancy, but you wouldn't listen," to Greg on multiple occasions.

One evening, it all came to a head. A knock on the door came, and it was Greg's mother and sister. While his sister rushed through the door and up the stairs, nearly knocking Nancy over the process, Greg stepped outside to talk to his mother.

Shortly after, Greg's sister rushed back out with a rolling suitcase and duffel bag in hand. When Nancy questioned her, with a smirk, she replied, "Greg is leaving you."

Her attempt to talk to Greg was thwarted when she realized her husband was already in the passenger seat of his mother's truck. Before Nancy knew it, they were taking off.

Struck with confusion, grief, and sorrow, Nancy stood on the porch watching it all. Hearing the phone ring, Nancy rushed to it in hopes of a call from Greg. Maybe he would explain what was going on? Would he tell her everything was going to be okay? Is he coming back soon?

But it wasn't Greg. Instead, it was Nancy's mother. Perhaps her motherly intuition tipped her off to make the call to check in.

Before either of them knew it, Nancy's mother was driving 15 hours to be at the side of her daughter; to help her through this awful event.

With her mother there, Nancy began seeking mental health treatment. The situation had become that dire. Grateful for her mother, she was able to become conscious of her burdens and willing to seek needed help.

Even so, the desire to call Greg was there. She wanted so badly to tell him she missed him – wanted him to call and let her know everything was okay. Without as much as a "goodbye," the man she married and loved had left home to live with his parents. It had been three weeks since that fateful evening on the porch. Her numerous calls to him remained unanswered.

Finally, out of the blue one evening, Greg called. His voice sounded tired, but he asked to meet for lunch the next day. Of course, Nancy would oblige. This was what she'd been waiting for, for nearly a month. At the restaurant, Greg broke down. He acknowledged his wrongdoing, expressing he felt as if he let himself and his wife down.

Diners stared as Greg's chest heaved with uncontrollable sobbing. "You're my wife, and you're important to me," he exclaimed. "My mother overstepped her bounds when she interfered in our marriage, and I failed you too on many levels."

It was there in the restaurant, Greg begged for Nancy's forgiveness.

Come to find out, Nancy's mother-in-law had high hopes for Greg to *never* return to Nancy. Reunited though, the two began to work through their troubles.

It had been months since Greg had moved back in and life was showing some semblance of normalcy when Nancy started noticing some weird symptoms. She'd feel some intense pressure while she peed. At times, she'd have pelvic pain; then came the sexual discomfort.

Of course, the last thing she wanted was for something else to come between her and Greg, so she consulted a doctor. At 26 years old, Nancy was told she had three large fibroids, the size of *tennis balls* on her uterus – she needed surgery immediately.

Thankfully for Nancy, the procedure went well with Greg by her side as she rested up. Then things got interesting again.

Through the chitter-chatter of friends and family in the waiting room, she noticed Greg's mother come in, but she wasn't alone. Alongside her, was a beautiful young lady. According to Greg's mother, it was "the beautiful young lady I told you about."

Right here. In this instance, with Nancy bedridden in a hospital, Greg's mother was continuing to try and ruin their marriage by setting him up with this woman.

Not once did the old hag ask about Nancy or visit her bedside.

During Nancy's recovery, Greg's mom beckoned him always. It seemed as if she was trying to keep him from Nancy. In typical Greg fashion, he would drop anything at her call. He simply couldn't stand up to her. Her manipulation had gotten so deep within him it was unbearable.

Then came what felt like a miracle.

Just months after surgery, Nancy got the greatest, yet most terrifying news of her life: she was pregnant. The couple seemed to be reborn once again, beside themselves with joy. But she knew what was ahead, and she knew Greg's mom would be a pain in the ass during this time.

For months, she dealt with negativity and rude behavior from Greg's mother, and then it happened: a baby boy was born. Greg was beside himself with pride and joy for this spitting image of himself. A celebration ensued with the family at the hospital chapel.

Fast-forward little more than a year, and another big announcement came. Nancy and Greg were expecting twins! But it wouldn't be without issue with Greg's mother.

Her relationship with Nancy had become even more strained by this time, and once the twin girls were born, Greg's mom insisted they be named after her. She called the names Greg and Nancy agreed on "ridiculous" and said they "had no meaning to her."

To Nancy's surprise, Greg stood up to his mother, putting her in her place and reprimanding her for continually belittling his wife. Still, his mother was relentless.

There in the hospital room, holding her twin grandchildren for the first time, she began calling them by the names she preferred and even sang them joyously, against Greg and Nancy's wishes.

While time tends to change things, people, and situations, it didn't this time.

Even a few years later, Greg's mother still harassed Nancy about everything from how she fed her children to the schools they attended. Little did she know, though, Greg was about to drop a bombshell on his dear mother.

You see, once the twins came along, Nancy stopped working to take care of the kids full-time. The family was financially on the ropes, so Greg took to the job market, looking for more gainful employment. He found it – out of state. For six months, Greg returned home every two weeks while looking for a home for the family in what would become their new state.

Once he did, his mother was livid. She didn't like how far the grandkids would be from her *or* how close they'd be to Nancy's family. Not one to be outdone, the old retiree started building her next plan to interject herself into their lives once more. With so much free time, she'd visit their new home frequently – *too* frequently.

But Nancy took it all in stride. Her life was improving with the distance between their family and Greg's mother, so rather than make her visits miserable, she decided to bury the hatchet with her. She spoke openly about feeling mistreated by her mother-in-law, who naturally took offense to everything said.

But Nancy kept calm. Her mother-in-law even showed some appreciation for her efforts; although she never once apologized for her monstrous behavior.

Soon, it would be Christmas. While excitement was bountiful, there was also some trepidation about traveling to Greg's parents' home for the holiday. But before the holidays could be observed, there was something Nancy had needed to address with Greg.

You see, Nancy was suspicious Greg was having an affair. Call it her "womanly intuition," but she was on edge even though on the outside, Greg gave the appearance of a loving, faithful husband and father. The topic had come up before, with Greg dismissing the "rumors." After all, they'd been together 15 years by now.

But when Nancy started noticing some irregularities in the laundry, her suspicion heightened. She'd find the occasional lipstick remnants on a shirt collar; at times a bit of foundation as well. These items, she'd pack away for future use.

One night after dinner, she brought it up again, which led to Greg denying everything once more... yet she didn't mention her findings because of how close it was to Christmas.

So, she dropped the matter. But as the fateful drive to Greg's parents' home approached, tensions mounted between the two. Once to their destination, they put the kids to bed. That's when Greg requested Nancy join him in driving to the store for supplies. It was on this drive, Greg admitted to Nancy he'd been out for a few drinks on three separate occasions with the same lady his mother brought to the hospital while Nancy recovered from surgery. But Greg said he'd stopped the relationship before it had gotten any further.

Throughout it all, Nancy never mentioned the shirts; perhaps she was too busy thinking about spending the holidays with a woman who was hell-bent on destroying her marriage.

~~

Made in the USA
Coppell, TX
04 October 2021